Late in the Midnight Hour

A MESSAGE OF FAITH DURING THE DARK HOURS OF OUR STORMS

Reverend Michael Gamble

WESTBOW
PRESS®
A DIVISION OF THOMAS NELSON
& ZONDERVAN

WestBow Press books may be ordered through booksellers or by contacting:

WestBow Press
A Division of Thomas Nelson & Zondervan
1663 Liberty Drive
Bloomington, IN 47403
www.westbowpress.com
844-714-3454

Scripture taken from the King James Version of the Bible.

ISBN: 978-1-6642-1325-8 (sc)
ISBN: 978-1-6642-1326-5 (e)

Print information available on the last page.

WestBow Press rev. date: 01/04/2021

To Shirley

I am blessed to have you by my side, and I could never imagine having anyone else in my life. I need you with me, always and forever. I know I can say anything in front of you, and you will never judge me. Thank you for being with me, my heart will always belong to you.

You are the love of my life and I can't imagine living in this world without you. You brighten each day and I feel so blessed. I am a blessed man to have you by my side, and I could never imagine having anyone else in my life. I need you, always and forever.

Contents

Introduction

One morning I woke up and opened the blinds of a window, I happened to look out and saw a group of senior citizens about seventy to eighty years old who live in the community, were on a morning walk. I said to myself, "will I be able to do that when I get to their age?" Do I know if I will see tomorrow? Sometimes, when things do not go our way or as plan, we lose faith, not only in ourselves but in the outcome of our nation especially during these unsettled times. It is easy to lose hope in things we do, things we plan, or past experiences, so how do we go on?

Faith, deep in its primary is rooted in expectations of good things to arise. It goes beyond hope. I saw faith in these senior citizens knowing that they will make it back to where they began their walk. While hope lives in my mind, the spirit of faith is in the heart it cannot be explained by rationality or to be unspoken or understood. While life can be hard on us at times, we must rely on faith, which to some can get very deep to understand and to others it is plain knowledge. It is a simple life that can be difficult if we do not have faith.

When we go to bed at night, how do we know in the morning we will rise to welcome a new day? Is it "Faith"? Some take it for granted that God's power will always be a part of our lives...

If anyone ever flew on a plane 35,000 feet in the air, we go from one minute to the next, wondering if we have enough faith that nothing will happen to the plane during its flight. Without faith, we could not expect things could turn out with no problems no matter what our situation may be. It is important to pray through the good and the bad, day or night and especially before you go to sleep.

So, what happens before we go to bed at night after a day of uncertainty? We worry, pacing the floors, and up all night trying to figure out a solution to our situation. Faith is as important as the air that we breathe. Although oxygen in the air nourishes the body, faith nurtures the soul. It is part of every force and every element of thought.

God does work while we sleep. When we give God the glory anyway possible, we are craving for his help, he hears every groan and work diligently to solve our problems as he blesses us. God already knows what we need, what our desires are, why we cry, and why we worry, he is just waiting for us to ask him, lean on him for help, this is where faith steps in. Without faith we cannot please God if we do not believe in him, we will not receive the blessing and the help we need. People who live by faith as followers of Christ are called believers. Are you a believer?

Looking back over our lives it is amazing how we have weathered, rough roads, bad storms, and life's daily mishaps. But for those who have served a mighty God we can see the evidence of God's incredible, grace, mercy, and power. We have experienced, known and felt the power of God in our lives as he sustained us through extremely difficult times. As a believer it took some time for me to trust that God will take care of me, forgive me, and love me, for all that I have done in the past and today. I am not perfect, we are not perfect, but God is perfect, he deserves to judge us, he is the only one with the authority to judge us. But in this world today people do judge one another. The question is why? Is it because they want to shift negative vibes towards others to take the spotlight off themselves? Or do they just want to be mean to one another? Our judgments or our assumptions about others must not insult them, must be genuine and must safeguard their characters. Yet, there are times we must assess another person's actions, mindsets, and performance. We do this when we vote, as leaders in a church, or when we recognize misleading or false teachers. This book is design to navigate us to a higher level of faith, trust, and belief in God. We must understand that faith moves. We cannot purchase it, sell it, or give it to our friends. The dictionary defines faith as "belief in, devotion to, or trust in somebody or something, especially without logical proof." The bible states that faith is belief in the one, true God without seeing Him. It is not neutral or non-committal. Without expressing faith and trust in God, we have no place with Him.

Intimate parts of my story in this book were told to allow access of a person that is not perfect, and that you are not alone in this Spiritual War. Everyone has a past that they may not be proud of, just remember

God allowed your past to happen for his Glory, remember it is not about you nor I. Wherever you are, whatever you are doing in your life I pray this book inspires you to continue to trust in the Lord, give him your all and that your destiny awaits. Best wishes to you as you endeavor into this exciting dimension of Christian life.

Acknowledgements

I never thought I would write a book. Even in college writing was hard because I wasn't into writing. I wanted to write about God but writing about Faith, the Bible, and my life experiences, seemed so far away because I needed encouragement. When I started to write sermons overseas in the Iraqi War, I wrote about what I felt about the Gospel.

I want to express my appreciation to my wife, Shirley who supported not only this book, but everything that I do. You have been with me through rough roads, bad storms, and life's daily beat downs you are more than wonderful; I love you always and thank you. To my children, Gabriel, Johnathon, and Martiece, my son-in-law finally my granddaughter my (ladybug) Zhuri thank you for the inspiration, you've made me wiser and stronger. My Capella University friends, and my HRC family thank you.

A special thank you to my Pastor Harold H. Craig Jr. for your mentorship and guidance. To the members of Morning Star Missionary Baptist Church, Radcliff Kentucky, To my mother Ella, Father Otis, sister Martrell, brother-in-law Tim brother Marland and all my in-laws, thank you for treating me like family it really has inspired me to grow.

To my fallen soldier Private First Class MichaelAngelo Mora, that night during combat you became our hero, thank you! I know you are watching over us, Rest in Peace. TiAnthony L. Wagner thank you for the friendship and inspiration, you were there for me during my health crisis, you taught me not to give in and do not give up. To the rest of my family and host of friends, you know who you are, I want to thank you because there is no me without you.

Chapter 1

God Answers Prayers

When we feel consume with trials and tribulations, it is a blessing that we have a chance to go to God in prayer and when we do, and nothing happens we sometimes lose faith; we lose hope in God. That is not part of the plan. What do we do next? We should continue to trust God and do his work. We also should continue to pray, fast, study his word trust that God is going to provide for us. He is not going to ignore us. What God want for children is good enough for us, he will not steer us in the wrong direction, just trust and believe him. Why? Because I tried him, and I know that it worked.

We live in a physical world with its four known space-time dimensions which are length, width, height, and time. Nevertheless, God abides in a different dimension, the spirit realm beyond the awareness of our physical senses. It is not that God is not real, it is that he is not limited by the physical laws and dimensions that govern out world.

John 4:24 said, "For God is Spirit, so those who worship him must worship in spirit and in truth" Go to him truthfully, pour out your heart, give him everything you have to offer and don't hold back. It will turn around for the good, it will be in your favor. Now be patient, it may take one day, one week, one month or a year, but don't give up because God want to see if you are going to be patient and wait for him and he want to bless you in this domino effect, every blessing that falls into your lap, will connect to another blessing that will fall into your lap, connecting to another blessing and so on. God's timing is incredible that way. The pieces must fall together.

You are praying for unanswered prayers and you are wondering since there are so many scriptures about answered prayers. Does God hear them? Is he going to answer my prayers? Let us go deeper!!!!!

> Mark 11:24
> "Therefore, I tell you, whatever you ask in prayer, believe that you have received it, and it will be yours."

> 1 John 3:22"And whatever we ask we receive from him, because we keep his commandments and do what pleases him."

> 1 John 5:14-15
> "And this is the confidence that we have toward him, that if we ask anything according to his will, he hears us. And if we know that he hears us in whatever we ask, we know that we have the requests that we have asked of him."

> 1 John 5:14-15
> "And this is the confidence that we have toward him, that if we ask anything according to his will, he hears us. And if we know that he hears us in whatever we ask, we know that we have the requests that we have asked of him.

God answers all prayers in his own time and in his own way. His answer would be, (Yes, No, or Not Yet) to our answered and unanswered prayers. It depends on your mindset how you are going to take the outcome of his answer. "Patience is the key to get through this". "Are you asking for the wrong thing? Only God will address that to you.

Many of us have pressed our way through times like these with some scars that are testimonies of the power of God in our lives. One thing I know for sure, when things do not go the way we think they should go, we question God's love for us. If homes, children, marriages, jobs, careers, family situations and circumstances are out of control, and we ask ourselves, "why isn't life turning out like I want it to?" We are at the point that we must decide if we are going to get bitter or go for victory, it is your choice.

In Psalms 90:4 Moses used a simple yet insightful analogy in describing the timelessness of God. He said, "For a thousand years in your sight are like a day that has just gone by, or like a watch in the night." The eternity of God is dissimilarity to man. You are doing all of the right things, going to church every Sunday, you join the choir, volunteer in the youth ministry, soup kitchen, nursing home facility, you volunteer to minister to inmates in a detention center, volunteer in the church kitchen and you even clean the church. Your schedule is full, and the words "ALL CHURCHED OUT" to the song, "Take Me to the King" by Tammela Mann has played constantly in your head. So, what is next in your church life with God? You say, "How do I get on God's good side. How do I pray and get those prayers answered? I am going to treat everyone right, I will not say a sentence with profanity, I even want to donate some of my personal things that I do not need to someone in need.

It's not enough to think of ways God wants us to be, he wants us to be natural enough that we do for him automatically and he is in our life naturally and that we do every that involves Christian life at a normalcy. We teach our kids everything we could and want everything for them that we did not have. So what do we do next?

I recall as kids, my sister 6 years old and I, about 11years old were invited to a neighbor's house for one of their kid's birthday party, my mother could not attend with us because she had to work, she really did not want us to go without her, but the neighbor insist that we attend. So my mother, in her strictest voice, gave us the speech about being nice and polite and she said, "Don't go over to that neighbor's house acting crazy like you don't have home training destroying their house and your better be listen to them, and don't let them tell me you were not good or you will have to answer to me." Not like God who is everywhere, even when we cannot see him, he is there, and he knows everything. Be a Christian because we must answer to God someday.

Do not stop praying or believing, be more personal with God, as the title of this book states "Late In the Midnight Hour" because one day ends at the same time another begins at the stroke of Midnight welcoming a new day. It's almost like New Year's Eve into New Year's Day. It is a special time to share a moment with "God". Praying at Midnight may not be the opportune time for you, but most importantly spend time with him.

Have patience with God because he is patient with us after all the things we have done or been through, we are still here, still standing, still above ground. Listen, I do not know what you are going through or been through, only God knows, therefore construct, and maintain a relationship with God and pour your heart out to him. He is available and know how much it is hurting you and how much you need him. Humble yourself and Embrace God's kindness to you. Feel free to come to Him in prayer just as you are. Expect Him to warmly welcome you and give you all the grace you need to overcome the suffering in your life.

Chapter 2

It is Just a Matter of Time

I don't know what you are going through, but I do know what I am going through or facing from day to day, but the Lord said, if you pray and pray with constant faith, it's just a matter of time before he open up doors in your life that no man can shut…It's just a matter of time before you are restored and your relationships with members of your family and friends are restored…. It is just a matter of time before your body and soul are healed… It is just a matter of time before you receive your answer…. It is just a matter of time before you receive victory. After that prayer, you will not be crying anymore, you won't be worried anymore, you won't be stressed anymore.

Those with broken hearts after a stressed situation, God will heal your heart. You have been waiting, you have been worrying, you have been feeling abandon, you have been feeling forgotten, But God said if you run to me and hold that relationship with me, you won't be rejected, you won't feel betrayed, you won't feel let down. God is going to show you exactly who he is. He is a good God, he is a merciful God, an understanding God, and an on-time God. Before you receive a problem, he already has the answer, praying is the topping on the cake for God.

Have you ever felt like you were facing a Giant in your life? Well God will fight that giant for you if you let him, you don't have to do anything but ask God to fight your battles. He already has a plan for you. It's just a matter of time before you walk into your victory. Before you receive that answer you have been praying about, he already had you on his mind. It's just a matter of time before he saves your loved ones, it's just a matter of time before he restores what is broken whether it is drugs or alcohol God can and will restore what is not right in your life. Sometimes we wait in fear if something or someone in our life will be destroyed. We get consumed in worry and try to fix it. We try to figure out a plan, God said, "if you wait on me, I will renew your strength".

Just trust in him, he will open doors that no man can shut. I want to encourage you to keep fighting, keep praying, keep praising, keep believing and trusting in his word. As a boxer in the ring, everything changes with one swing, one punch, one night and one praise. When we hold a relationship with God, he places us on a different course that will change the rest of our lives. One thing about the devil he will lie and make things seem ok when we know that it is not. The devil lies about your marriage, about your dreams, about your children, relationship, and your jobs. He is the enemy, and he cannot win. The Lord said pick up that towel and toss it back at the devil and get back into the fight. God will put you in a predicament only he can get you out. And when he gets you out of it, it will prove to you, that you know what you know about God.

The devil wants you to be bitter, if your soul is bitter, how can you prosper? How can you be free to think your best thoughts? All your energy is being expended in the kayos you are living. You will not have the focus to win and change to be better. Therefore, change so that your mind can be renewed and that you can be there for your family. It is a matter of time for a change for your life. We must keep the faith during the storm.

Chapter 3

Just Believe in Him

In chapter 2, we talked about it's just a matter of time before you receive victory just believe. Belief is an especially important thing knowing that you will receive victory, it's not just a matter of being in a part of a group, a tribe, a click or a cult. Belief has all to do with your philosophy that you live by your vision, your purpose, and your goals. As Christians we come to understand or we should understand that what God is most concern about is "BELIEF", believing in him. He said, I know you're weak, I know you've made mistakes, I know you go astray along the way but, if you believe in me it is counted unto you as righteousness.

God wants you to believe to survive what you are going through; he is offering you a solution to your problems so that you can reach your destiny. God wants you to ask for what you need. The absolute best of us fall short of the righteousness of God. I do not care how much of a stuffed shirt some people are or trying to act super holy. God is real and we must be accountable to him.

God said to Abraham, "I will count you as being righteous even though you are not righteous just because you believe in me". "Abraham believe God", the bible said, and it was counted until him as righteousness. Just because he believed in God. That is why you must be careful about judging people. Sometimes the one doing the judging might not be on the books as well as the one you are judging because God counted that person's belief as righteousness. God is most concerned that we believe in him. We must walk in truth and clarity, we see people walking around with T-shirts with crosses, carrying bibles bigger than center blocks and chains with large crosses. This does not mean much as to talking and believing his word and walking in God's light. If you trust and believe in his word, it will work out for the Good. Shortly after I retired from the Army, I was diagnosed with anxiety and Post traumatic Stress Disorder with depression. I was depressed for a while and could not understand what was going on with me, I could not identify myself as depress. Does this sound familiar? With prayer and God's grace, today I am under doctor's care and I am finally doing better.

The enemy does what he can to destroy our belief system. If I open a business it should have a vision, purpose, and goals because the customers are entitled to know that this is who I am. I am defined by my vision, my purpose, and my goals. That is my playbook. That is my creed, that is my belief as a company. If you know who you are, then you know who you are not. If you do not know who you are, then somebody can describe any identity on you, then you will be what they want you to be. Does this make sense?

When bitterness gets down in side of you because nothing seems to work, you walk away from something good in your life, you walk away from your family, your friends and from your blessing, God says, "All things not some things, not most things, not big things nor small things, but all things will work out for the good of those who trust in the Lord." Have you been called to serve him"?

God does not cause trials, he allows them to happen, and when he does…he equips you to handle the situation why? Because it is according to his plan. And let us not forget he is God and in control. Your natural instincts cause you to do a quick fix. Quick fixes increase damage. Wanting to fix it yourself wanting to receive your harvest without conflict can cause more problems. When you ask God to help…'LEAVE IT ALONE', do not call anyone, do not text anyone, do not write anyone, and do not try to straighten things out yourself.

When you and I are in the middle of our sufferings or experiencing trials, it's like being able to see a little part of the puzzle, we can't begin to imagine how it could all fit together for our good. But God who is all wise and in perfect control sees the big picture and knows exactly how to make even our troubles work out for the good I am going to say this again!!!!

When you and I are in the middle of our sufferings or experiencing trials, it's like only being able to see a little part of the puzzle, we can't begin to imagine how it could all fit together for our good. But God who is all wise and in perfect control sees the big picture and knows exactly how to make even our troubles work out for the good! Sometimes, that good is reminding us to rely on his strength and not our own. Sometimes it is to give an opportunity to witness our faith to others, or to drive us back to his word so our faith is strengthened in hearing his promises. I really think it is to keep out priorities straight by reminding us that this life is temporary, and our ETERNAL LIFE is forever.

We cannot stop going to church because of our issues. We cannot hide out in our homes pulling the sheets over our heads or pacing the floors looking for answers. I hear excuses from time to time for example; I won't be coming to church because I did not like what that person said, I am not getting fed the word, or the excuse I heard the most is, I worked hard this week I need to rest I'll watch a sermon on T.V.

In (Acts Chapter 8:4) when the early church was being persecuted, it seemed like a bad thing, but the good out of it was the fact it made the Christians leave Jerusalem and take the gospel to other parts of the world, "But the believers who had fled Jerusalem went everywhere preaching the Good News about Jesus." We must go to church to weather our storms. If Jesus carried the cross to calvary for us, then we should be able to go to church to hear a word from God.

Someone said to me, "not all storms are bad, there are storms that clear the path for a blessing". As we go through storms, he is preparing us for greater. I know people say things, but I strongly believe that God is pruning us (getting us ready) for the greater good. We must go to a place and say, "NOT MY WILL, BUT YOUR WILL BE DONE." God does not always want to just do something "IN" us, but often His goal is to do something "THROUGH" us.

Saints, if you want to be a blessing to others, you must be broken. Remember, a vessel that is unbroken has limited use for others. As a believer we face trials and sometimes things do happen, but if we are faithful to the Lord, he will work it out for our good. In the bible God told Moses to read his book of instructions and do not go left or right. We must hold on to God's unchanging hand, it will all work out. We must keep the faith during our storm.

Chapter 4

My Condition is not
my Conclusion

Before I enlisted in the Army, during my 12th grade year in high school, while living at home with my parents, I wanted to get a job, I only needed one credit to graduate, so I signed up for a work study program to get a job. I went on the hunt for this job, went into a shoe store applied for the job, was interviewed, and got the job and was now a shoe salesman in a Men's Shoe Store in the Mall. After graduating I continue to work in the store and became an excellent salesman. After a couple of years, I became the manager and that is when my life became difficult.

I had management power and was doing my own thing. I became good friends with some employees at an adjacent store. We would party after work. Drugs became a quick and expensive habit and I started excessive spending to support my habit. It was getting bad, but I thought that I could control it. My shoe inventory was short, and the store became out of hand things were out of sorts. I ended up borrowing from friends to pay the shortages in the store. I would make my own hours, working 2 to 3-hour days, I was out of control.

I could not see myself there much longer. I said to myself, "I need to move on before I find myself in jail." I applied for a job with the postal service and got the job. I then gave my two weeks' notice at the shoe store and began working at the distribution postal center working night shifts.

My habit got stronger and more frequent everyone there was doing drugs. We would get off in the mornings, all of us would go to an after-work party where the drugs and alcohol were plentiful, and this was a consent thing. I got no sleep all day until it was time to go to work again. Sometimes I would be up for 48 hours straight. If I ever thought I needed God, it would be now. I never thought I had a problem, I never thought it would get out of hand, but it did.

My parents started noticing something, I was acting different, my siblings were concerned. Everyone thought I would be going to work but, I did not show up. I would call in making excuses. A different excuse every day. Meanwhile, I would be driving all night around the neighborhoods in the bad part of town getting into things.

As my mother and father continue to voice their concerns about me, I was losing my job. As a last attempt to keep my job, the postal service agreed to send me to a rehab facility. Things were changing in my life. Something inside of me erupted and I started to see what drugs were doing to me, mentally and physically. It was in there, I started praying wanting this to work.

I went back to work at the post office, it was a struggle going back, I wanted to make my sobriety work, I needed to make it work, I needed to go back to when my mother would take us to church and pray for a word from the Lord, I needed him to focus on me. After six months, I "RELAPSE", Because I did not try hard enough to be with God, I lost the need for praying, I lost myself through the madness. Not to mention I lost my job, lost my car, my self-esteem, and the respect of my family, I was lost.

One of the things I love about the Lord is that it doesn't matter what you've done in your life, it doesn't matter how many mistakes you've made, if it wasn't for the blood of Jesus. If it was not for the blood... I was so messed up, the good thing is, I have been washed by his blood. The only comfort we have is the fact that God is in Control, he is on the throne, and if he is on the throne I do not know how things are going to work out, but I know it will work out. He has it already worked out. It does not make a difference if it does not work out the way I want it too. If it works out the way God wants it too, it is alright with me.

One night I was walking the neighboring streets in 30-degree weather with no coat looking for drugs with five dollars in my pocket. Fortunately

I was not successful in finding drugs, it was a long walk back home, Once I got home to my parent's house, I laid on the bed looking at the ceiling, something came over me, tears began to roll down the corners of my eyes down my face I contemplated a thought of suicide and I have placed everything on the line because I had nothing else to lose, Satan has made his point. It seemed ridiculous, a grown man living at home with his parents, no car, no job, and no future. I wanted to let go. Within minutes I fell asleep.

Morning came it was 7:10am after a restful sleep, I awaken to God giving me the strength, giving me peace, and giving me my life. A second after opening my eyes, I turned my head and focused my eyes on the yellow page book on the night stand, at first my goal was to look for a job, as I opened the yellow pages I flipped the pages right to the Army Recruiter section without planning. Was it a sign from God, "I thought"? If my prayer was to be answered, if I needed to renew my mind and my life, I had to trust God. I needed to trust in his word.

Knowing that he would not fail me, he gave me peace, he gave me hope, he gave me my life. I knew then that I was safe, and that God loved me, I knew he cared, so I had to press my way through this. It was a critical time in my life, God wanted me to start my life over, I had to leave my old neighborhood and the dangerous streets. Starting a new chapter in my life was part of the plan, and that I did. I needed a relationship with God in my new life's chapter. So I joined the Army and got out of the neighborhood when I realized I am a fighter, I am not going to quit… leave the past in the rear view mirror because my condition is not my conclusion…….

Chapter 5

Faith and the Military

S o I am in the Army at twenty three years old...Through countless training exercises and deployments into war, I knew that God would work things out for me, he will make a way for me to return home, but it did not stop me from worrying. I was scared, I did not know what to expect, although my family was 10,000 miles over the waters I continue to read scriptures, inspirational books and pamphlets, and I prayed and spoke to God often. I found myself in the middle of these big fight in Iraq. I experienced fear, stress, depression, and anxiety but it was no time to breakdown.

We fought and killed countless Iraqi insurgents in multiple towns, roadblocks and when they attacked our convey, there were days we fought 9am to 5pm. We would hear of soldier's dying from other units but no time to mourn. After a long day of fighting, at the end of the day I brushed off the war fighting dust and prepared to get a night's sleep. This would go on for weeks but before I laid down to sleep, during "MIDNIGHT", I made it my point to talk to God, I asked him to keep us close to him, I am a leader and had to lead, I asked God to hold me together, to hold us all together there was no time to show feelings I wanted him to build a fence of protection around us everywhere and for us to do what we were there for.

Whenever it was time for us to depart our camp for a combat mission, I thought that it may be a possibility that some or all of us may not make it back to camp alive, so as we depart the camp, I would pray with my crew and each time we depart I had someone to pray so each crew member got the chance to talk briefly to God asking him to give us courage and peace. As I look back during the War, I wanted my crew to try and be a little more spiritual to connect with God. I did not want to force Religion on my crew but to give them a peace to go to during our tough days.

At night while everyone was in their bunk areas asleep, we all spent time saying something to God, it would be midnight quiet time, no moving around which seemed the best time to receive a word from God. I was proud to start my soldiers on the journey with God. Along with regular prayer, my midnight one on one with God was personal. I felt so good, so protected, so secure like I feel today, safe in his arms. Not that I never felt it before, it was or is a special time with God. I did this during all my combat deployments and field training exercises This became a regular thing and I've hoped my soldiers continued talking with God even when we return home….

Being in the Military was not always a fun ride at the park, during the down times I really needed a word from God to get me back on track. There were times I felt alone, a meltdown, I felt lost in a world that no one could understand. Sometimes I reflected on past indiscretions and go into a slight depression but had no time to stay in it long because I had work to do. Have you ever felt like you wanted to break down but could not for important reasons? There have been a few times I have, but God took me to a place to feel his presence and to stay the course. God created this incredible plan for me.

As a retired Service member today, I continue to work, working for the Military but as a civilian I realized that God was and still is in charge of my life and that he provided this job for me to give soldiers spiritual and career guidance, as well as personal guidance. His work continues and I am a witness to tell someone that there is only one God, a living and true God, he is an intelligent, spiritual, and personal Creator, Provider, Preserver and Ruler, he has given me approval to evangelize while helping soldiers as well as anyone who were in need of some encouragement in the word. It is hard being in the military today than it was since I came in back in the 80's. If I could give a little advice at any time, it is worth it all.

God is a perfectionist all-knowing and a powerful ruler. Through all combat tours and exercises I had to push my way through it all knowing that God was there to guide me and today he is still covering me. He led us out of danger and placed me in his care and the arms of comfort. When I think about the goodness of Jesus and all that he has done for me, he stood by me watching me make mistakes along the way and he picked me up when I fell. He kept me from being hurt while in danger, he even kept me from harming myself and for that I thank him because when it looked like I wasn't going to make it, he turned the tables and showed me that only he can do the impossible. Remember if you are in the military now, you can do this. You can press your way through anything the military has thrown your way.

I enlisted in the Military to serve my country first; it was hard at first when I became involved in the intense training, military life, the gulf war, and Iraqi War this became harder and more difficult. I knew that God construct this plan no matter where I am or where I go, but I was being called to minister. I can feel God and know that he forgave me for my transgressions, therefore I wanted the privilege to preach. I had and still have access to the throne at any time and could enter God's presence through prayer and my worship. At war time I had no temple to go to, so my temple to praise him was within me. There is no excuse to worship wherever you go. We must make the time and the place for the Lord no matter where we are.

Chapter 6

Though I Walk Through the Midst of Trouble

God has stretched his hands out to all of us at some time in our lives. He stretched it against anger, health issues, stress, evil, wrongdoing, and backstabbing to say the least. And with his right hand he saved us. The Lord has vindicated us, your God did not abandon us. I realize when I was in the streets doing, as my mother would say, "no good", I never thought about God, I only thought about me, but he still love me.

In the bible David was a man who walked into trouble all the time. His Psalms express the struggles and disappointments he faced. But at the end he always focuses his energy on God. The Key is the victory and his attitude which is deemed in his strong faith in God. This is what we need to do, grab a hold of the victorious attitude of faith in ourselves and focus it to God. David was assured in God's purpose. That is why he said, "The Lord will accomplish what concerns me" He will take care of your concerns. The only way we can walk through trouble, trials and situations is keeping the focus on God. He promises to do good work in our lives. Therefore, when trouble arises, trust him to deliver. The way he can do this is in valleys of hardship. God takes all responsibility in what concerns us. That is why he can say "Yes or No"

I want to encourage someone who reads this book that it does not matter what answer you get from the Lord; it will be the right answer, it will set the foundation of trust between ourselves and him. You may not like the answer you get, but you will survive. I believe that God can miraculously alter a bad situation for anyone if we just pray asking him for a miracle and be patient it will come to pass.

He is a true God, he is the essence of truth because there is no one like him (2 Samuel 7:21-22) he is the same, yesterday, today and for eternity. His perfect will is eternal, so we do not have to worry about shifting values. Because he is truth, we know that he will never lie to us. He has proven himself to us to be faithful so as we walk through trouble times, we must know that God is trustworthy because he is in control of every situation.

I recall cigarette smoking while overseas. I was in the Iraqi War, it was the thing to do, a peer pressure soldier thing. It seems like everyone was doing it and I believe that it seemed to calm the nerves, and then I became hooked on it. When I returned home from the war, my kids did not know about my habit of smoking cigarettes. I would go outside in the back yard to smoke, after I was done, I would run inside and straight to the bathroom, brush my teeth, wash my hands and around my mouth then spray on a little cologne to cover up the smell keeping it away from my kids, as of today my kids never mention if they knew or not. I became tired of the smoking routine, so I ask God, to deliver me from smoking and to somehow take the taste of cigarettes from my mouth. And in two weeks he made it happened, and twenty five years later "no smoking" just like that.

Does the situation sound a little familiar? We as Christians, hide what we do and cover it up when we are in church. Nothing can prevent God from attaining his picture-perfect will. If we want God to move in our direction, we must concentrate on what we want God to take care of.

When I was diagnosed with cancer, at first it hit me like a falling rock, then I cried, then I got mad, and went right into denial. Then God said, "Are you finish?" "I am going to get the Glory from this". I had to make sense of the why me, so I thought, he wanted me to be a blessing to someone who maybe going through a health or situational crisis like me. The only option I had was surgery and I did not hesitate with the surgery it was because I trust that it was God's will. He placed the answer in my head without a doubt.

After surgery I awakened and received the word that the cancer was successfully removed, I was relieved it was over, God got his Glory! The recovery was a little difficult and uncomfortable at first, but I still gave God the praise for taking the cancer and not me. I learn from this health crisis that you must be broken; you must trust God and to be a blessing to others. I am a different person today, a working progress because God cared enough to deliver me even with my flaws, my indiscretions, and my sins, he still blessed me.

Remember, nothing can prevent God from achieving his perfect will. Regardless of how difficult our troubles may seem to us. He is a power worker, a miracle worker, a faithful worker. As God's children we will be affected by trouble, we will consume tribulations, we will suffer from stress, we will be affected by anger, and in distress from the daily beat downs of life, but remember God with his awesome wisdom and unending love has our backs. We must keep the faith during the storm.

Chapter 7

Holy Spirit and It's Power

The Holy Spirit and its power are ours and it lives within us. God wants us to take risk with the Holy Spirit. Step out in obedience. There are somethings we can be confident about and that is the Holy Spirit. He gives us divine strength to be victorious. When we stumble, he holds us up, and when we fall, he gives us refuge. The Holy Spirit is not a Ghost but is misunderstood in the church today. We cannot live a Christian life without God, and we should not try. You cannot control the Holy Spirit; you can quench it and welcome it but cannot control it. There is no passage in the bible that states that only through the Holy Spirit is faith possible, Holy Spirit produce faith, it happens through the word of God spoken by inspired leaders of God, the Apostles.

The Holy Spirit guides us and welcomes us to participate in worship, we must believe that the Holy Spirit is especially important for our spiritual growth. God is much concern about our belief in the Holy Spirit and in him. Some of us go astray along the way but, if you can believe in the father it is counted unto you in righteousness. The Holy Spirit is part of our worship, part of our praise. The Holy Spirit can surprise a person during worship; it can sneak up on you fast and can be uncontrollable at best.

Being involve in church, I can say that I have experienced many things good and bad even a strong case of the Holy Ghost Spirit a few times while in and outside of church. I felt closer to God during those times which mattered so much. While in the presence of God I could not say a word or make a sound and when I could, I would ask him to stay and that I did not want him to go. Have you ever wanted more of him? The Holy Spirit's power is ours. It lives within us and gives us the divine strength to be victorious. When we fall, he picks us up, and when we stumble, he maintains us.

Galatians 5:22-25 states "But the fruit of the Spirit is love, joy, peace, patience, kindness, goodness, faithfulness, gentleness and self-control. Against such things there is no law. Those who belong to Christ Jesus have crucified the sinful nature with its passions and desires. Since we live by the Spirit, let us keep in step with the Spirit." We must keep the faith during our storm.

Chapter 8

God Perform Miracles

Picture this! You've had a long week at work and there is a church program to go to on Friday night. You get off from work Friday evening and cannot wait to be there to praise and worship the Lord, to listen to worship songs while waiting for a word from the Lord. I recall back in the day before I turn my life completely over to God, Friday and Saturday nights would be club nights. I could not wait to get off from work. My friends and I would go to the liquor store, get dressed and go out. Looking back at those moments, I thought about nothing but having fun and partying. I never knew that one day I had to give it all up, in which at that time of my life was not negotiable and now be accountable to God. Instead of having what I called fun in liquored spirits, God made changes in my life and it was time to grow and concentrate on the Holy Spirit. The question was asked, when is it time to give God the glory, the honor, and the praise?

One of my close friends in the military who I used to party with and hung out with in Germany, is now married and a pastor of his own church. I smile today because I would never think to this day we would be where we are today. We were bad influences on each other back then. I never thought in a million years that we would be a working vessel for the Lord. We never thought about being Pastors and Ministers it was never in the cards.

God is a miracle worker. I can say, "It's just a matter of time"! When I contacted my old buddy recently, in which we haven't spoken in 20 years, we both laughed and talked about old times. We could not believe that we both settle down, got smart and put God first in our lives. If by any chance you think that it cannot or will not happen for you, I would say, "you are wrong, trust me, I've seen it happened" and I've experienced it. God does not make mistakes, it may not happen today, it may not happen next week or even next month, but it will happen.

One day while sitting around the house the thought came to pass of who I was then and who I am now, all I could do is smile and thank God for his greatness. We all should take inventory of our life past and present to see how far we've come. So, the miracle I was waiting for was in my mouth, meaning I had to ask to speak the existence and not doubt. I had to ask God to give me a better life, a life to do nothing but serve him.

The problem that most of us have is saying things we do not believe with our whole heart. The bible said, those who do not waver do not receive anything from God. Remember, Jesus told us to speak to the mountain, we should ask for what we want. As they say, "A closed mouth does not get fed". Jesus said, "I am the way, the truth and the light".

There are those that ask for things and expect to receive it right away from God. Guess what? God does things on his own time, within his own schedule. There are some people that think because they volunteer work at the nursing home, the soups kitchen, work with the youth department and even sing in the choir, that it entitles them to have first choice of the blessings and receive their blessing when they need it. Yes, God perform miracles, he performs prophecies that he fulfills which are our testimonies that Jesus is real, and he is alive, he has changed my life and he can change yours. God makes the choice when to bless you.

I have experienced God's love and joy in my life through the good and the bad. In the past I've made a mess with my life, what about you? I've disappointed people in my life, I've lost jobs, friends possessions and my self-esteem, my mind was out of control and I could not trust my heart. The bible says that a man thinks in his heart, that the way he is going. (Proverbs 23:7). It really does matter where you are with the Lord, the way you think is the way you will go with your life. I've experienced God's love, but my mind was not restored. I realize that you cannot have someone talk to you, hold your hand and to transform your mind. There are times when your experience has an impact on you, they do not always change your belief. You must have and hold a relationship with God, give him the chance to help you. We must keep the faith during our storm.

Chapter 9

You Are Not a Prisoner of Your Past

Romans 11:33-34 says Oh, the depth of the riches of the wisdom and knowledge of God! How unsearchable his judgments, and his paths beyond tracing out! Who has known the mind of the LORD? Or who has been his counselor? I have made some mistakes in my life, and when I look back at them, I welcome my past because those mistakes got me here today. One day I used drugs and alcohol all day, am I proud of it? No! I could feel my heart pounding out of my chest. I was not scared of an Overdose, crazy huh. I am careful to ask the question? How did I make it through that time in my life? I can say that I have experienced drugs and can boldly be a spokesperson for the slogan "Just Say No". If you are on a rollercoaster ride please get off and get on a spiritual ride with the Lord.

As a teenager going into my early twenties, I was on a bad rollercoaster ride. I respect my parents and disrespect my parents at the same time, I've argued, stormed out of their house and return in a couple of days. I was not responsible to be on my own. I know that sounds strange, but it is true. I was crazy that was true. I left home to live in my car just to get out of the house and to be on my own I did not want anyone spying on me or trying to give me the talk of my life I had no money, no dream, no plan, and no relationship with God. I still had a car but no money for gas, until one day the car was found by creditors and was repossessed. So, I had nothing

I hit rock bottom, it became midnight I recall deciding that I wanted to make a change I needed to talk to someone, that someone had to be God. I remember what my mother would tell us about God answering prayers, so I said, "here I am Lord, I am praying to you".

It is scary not knowing all the answers, it is more humbling to get on your knees and ask God for the answers, trusting in him and believing in him. The answers may not come right away but believe me it will come. Sometimes when the answer from God isn't clear, or you may not get all of it at one time, it is hard to understand God when he does not make the answer clear or when he does not answer your prayers in a timely manner. But what we do not understand is that whatever God decides for us, is for us.

It took me a while to trust in the Lord, I did not know what I needed to know about him. I knew nothing about reading the Bible, I did not know about the power God has. Just like trying new products, you must try them to see if they work. Well, I thought I had to try God to see if he was consistent in blessing me, I was desperate and did not know how God worked. But it is more to it, you must sustain a relationship with God and be that working vessel for him, spread his word, believe, and receive him and understand his work.

There were times when I wished I could rub that Aladdin's lamp to receive my blessing. I realize that actions have consequences even for Christians who follow the Lord. I also realize doing well does not make everything in your life great. Sometimes it can be the opposite. I have experienced the love of God, but my thinking was way off, and my mind was not renewed, therefore I was doing it all wrong in my life.

I used to worry about what I have done in the past, but it is useless because it is already done. Remember, never be a prisoner of your past, it is a lesson, not a life sentence. Worry about what is ahead tomorrow makes one more day anxious and stressful, so take the hint, and take careful steps, you want to do this right. I should be focusing on what is inside my heart. This means God is my heart, therefore I must know God. It is not a bad idea to read and absorb his word, which is absorbing him, let God saturate you with his grace and mercy, seek that relationship with him. Once I get my heart right with God, I can enjoy the blessings of just being.

I used to wake up in the morning feeling like I was fighting an opponent in the boxing ring, every swing, every blow seemed to connect to my body. When I wake, I felt tired, run down and my head hurt. I wonder if my opponent followed through with an upper cut to my head. Was it a knockout? It felt like it. When you go to bed at night with worry, stress, and unsettled pressure you wake up tired, powerless, and fearful. Allowing yourself to be engulfed in despair can be depressing. Where is God in all of this? Let us go deeper!

When we seek to journey with God, we must abandon our sense of self and embrace God's gracious offer of countless blessings. Therefore, we must as the song say, "have a little talk with Jesus, tell him all about our struggles". So, remember (midnight) do not go to bed with burdens, cast all cares upon him. Let God fight those battles, you get the sleep and let God work those miracles with success throughout the night. Just ask him, "God, help me to replace my fear with faith and overcome evil with good". I felt confident when placed in situations that felt like I was surrounded by hungry lions. In him I live, I move, and I have my spiritual peace. One of my favorite scriptures Act 17:28--For in him we live, and move, and have our being; as certain also of your own poets have said, for we are also his offspring. Remember your past is not your future.

Chapter 10

Grace and Mercy the Power of the Gospel

The good news is the power of the Oh Mighty God is continuous. This makes a person like me jump up and down and shout when getting that revelation about the magnitude of God's grace and mercy. The Gospel is good news, is like someone hitting the lottery kind of good news. Getting God's Grace and mercy will set you free because he is good to us. The book of Romans explains what God has done for us independently of what we deserve. In Romans, the Apostle Paul said that grace is the power revealing the righteousness of God. Remember this, mercy withholds a punishment we deserve; grace gives a blessing we do not deserve. The only way any of us can enter a relationship with God is because of his grace toward us.

> Hebrews 4:16, therefore, let us draw near with confidence to the throne of grace, so that we may receive mercy and find grace to help in time of need.

> 1 Corinthians 15:10, But by the grace of God I am what I am, and His grace toward me did not prove vain; but I labored even more than all of them, yet not I, but the grace of God with me.

Mercy is part of the personality of God, who wants it to be part of our character. Mercy is grace's effect on justice, and thus it is another side of justice. It is rooted in love: God shows mercy because God loves us and forgives us. Through grace and mercy, God offers those who do wrong a new chance to get it right. He is a second chance, God he gives us a second chance to get it right for some of us a third and fourth chance if we refuse to learn from our mistakes.

Ephesians states by grace we are saved by grace through faith. But if we seize to get saved, faith and grace will be out of balanced. Grace is what God does for us separate of what we deserve, grace is unearned Favor. God gives you grace preceding to you needing it. If I were to be worthy of grace to get God's grace then it would not be grace, then it would be a payment for the goodness I have done. Grace is all about God.

God's grace got me out of many situations because I had faith in him to help me through. Some people think that they need to hold on to God until they get what they want, again it does not work that way. Some say, I will ask God to heal me, I will have God bless me, I am going to ask God for that job. Faith does not make God do anything. If it was not done in the atonement phase of Jesus, then faith cannot make it happen. You cannot make God do anything such as healing you, he has already provided that through your faith.

> Mark 11:23-24 For verily I say unto you, That whosoever shall say unto this mountain, Be thou removed, and be thou cast into the sea; and shall not doubt in his heart, but shall believe that those things which he saith shall come to pass; he shall have whatsoever he saith. Therefore, I say unto you, what things so ever ye desire, when ye pray, believe that ye receive them, and ye shall have them.

This scripture declares that whatever you desire, when you pray, believe and you will receive, then you shall have it. Christians, we have a job to do a role to play. We must approach Faith with belief, we must gather and use what God has bestowed which is everything that has been determined by his grace.

When I was diagnosed with stage three prostate cancer, my first thought was why? Then I jumped right into, "I must take care of this now". I knew God had to get the glory from this because I was not worried about my condition. I figured I was placed on this earth for a reason and was chosen with this cancer for a reason. Therefore, I must make this cancer a healing statement. I cannot deny that I wasn't scared, but as time became closer for surgery I began to wonder if I was going to come out of this ok, that is what Satan wants in us, doubt. The disbelief that Satan tried to place in me, but God's Grace, Mercy, and his Power overcame the works of Satan.

Do not ever think that God has forgotten about you, in fact you are always on his mind. God will put you in a predicament, only he can get you out. And when he gets you out of it, it will prove to you, that you know what you know about God. Just remember in the book of Romans which states, all things work together for good to them that love God, to them who are called according to his purpose. There is a purpose behind everything that you are going through in life. But the revelation comes in stages of your life. We must keep the faith during our storm.

Chapter 11

"When there seemed to be nowhere to escape TRAPPED"

God called Moses to return to Egypt to set his people free. God Promised Abraham that he would become a great nation. This meant that God promised to make Abraham's descendants, the Israelites, a large and mighty nation. God always keeps his promises. There were many Israelites in Egypt, and that Pharaoh made them all slaves. God wanted to save his people, so he told Moses to go before Pharaoh and tell him to "Let My people go". Moses listened to God and agreed to go to Pharaoh.

Things did not start well for Moses, the first time Moses went to Pharaoh, and asked him to set the Israelites free, Pharaoh said "NO". Then Pharaoh made the slaves work even harder, the people complained against Moses, and he became discouraged. Moses took his discouragement to the Lord. God reminded Moses of his promises then told Moses that he would free the people and give them the land that he promised Abraham.

Moses led 600,000 people out of Egypt in the middle of the night. But God did not lead Moses and the Israelites through enemy land, rather he led them through the desert toward the Red Sea as they journeyed to the Promised Land. As Pharaoh's army came after Moses and the Israelites, it looked like an impossible situation. To the east was the seas, to the South and West were mountains, and to the North was Pharaoh's army. The Israelites were trapped. Let us picture this, To the North your bills, to the South, problems on the job, the East, the car broke down and to the west the family crisis…. "YOU ARE TRAPPED"

The Israelites were afraid, they were blaming Moses for being trapped. The interesting thing here is that God led them exactly to this place where they would feel trapped. He was about to show the entire world his amazing power as the one who rescues his people. So, the Lord spoke to Moses, "Why are you crying out to me?" Tell the people of Israel to move on. The Lord told Moses to stop praying and get moving, Prayer must have a vital place in our lives, but there is also a place for action. Sometimes we know what to do, but we pray for more guidance as an excuse to postpone doing it. If we know what to do, then be like "Nike", JUST DO IT!

There was no way to escape, but the Lord opened a dry path through the sea. When their backs were up against the wall, and it seemed like there is no way to control your situation, God can, and he will open a way. When we find ourselves caught in a problem and see no way out, do not panic God will open a way.

Obstacles can make a road hard to travel, whether there's a fender bender, pothole or fallen tree across that road, God will open up a way for you to continue your journey. Just remember this, "Not all storms come to disrupt your life, some come to clear your path". When a storm approaches your life, brace yourself and go through it holding onto God's unchanging hand. He will get you through it, God will saturate you with the strength and determination to press your way towards the finish line.

There is nothing too big or too small for God. There is nothing to be afraid of, you got this race, picture this: The finish line is in your line of sight, you are a few yards away, just lower your head, curve your back forwarded, and give it all you've got, lean in, it's all or nothing, before you know it, YOU'VE MADE IT! YOU FINISHED! The race is over, you've won against the devil's work. He thought he had you, but you've proved him wrong. The storm is over, you've made it through the hail, the flood, the lightening, the twister and now the calm.

What I am saying is that no matter how much you think you are outweighed or over your head with your struggles, your issues, your problems, or tribulations, God can and he will step right in and do what he said he would do, it has happened to me multiple times, he will step in that boxing ring and knock out your opponent, your situation and free you from your trials and get the Glory. All he wants us to do is believe and receive and spread the news on how he blessed you.

How many people get the blessings from God and will not tell it? As Christians we have the opportunity, the right, and the responsibility to tell someone about God's goodness. We do not have to buy tickets, nor would we have to stand in line to have a relationship with God. He is always available for us, reminding us of his words. We must keep the faith during the storm.

Chapter 12

God allowed it to happen

Understanding that God had allowed this to happen so that he could be a man of power in Egypt, Joseph said, "God turned to good what you [my brothers] meant for evil. He brought me to the high position I have today so I could save the lives of many people" (Genesis 50:20).

When the doctor came into the examination room after I have waited for 45 long minutes, he said Mr. Gamble you have cancer. I don't know if I was angry at him for the way he told me, or if I was angry at myself for the toxicants, drugs and cigarettes that I've ingested into my body for years. After it sunk in a while, I asked myself the question why me, a few times, I immediately answered, "Why not me"? God allowed me to take on this mission. God allows things to happen. God allows you to go through what you go through for a reason, for his glory. Have you ever asked God, "Why Me God"? When are you going to deliver this from me? The Apostle Peter reminded us, not to be surprised at the fiery ordeal that has come on you to test you, as though something strange were happening to you" (1 Peter 4:12). All of Jesus' followers experienced oppression.

So, the question I asked myself, Am I supposed to be exempt from hardships? To tell you that no one is exempt because trials which are merely unavoidable are an element of God's blueprint. We do not need to figure it out or seek to find wisdom in it because some things will be revealed to us and some won't.

Romans 8:28
And we know that God causes all things to work together for good to those who love God, to those who are called according to His purpose.

2 Corinthians 4:15
For all things are for your sakes, so that the grace which is spreading to more and more people may cause the giving of thanks to abound to the glory of God.

Ecclesiastes 3:1
There is an appointed time for everything. And there is a time for every event under heaven—

If God is so wonderful and caring, why does He allow evil? This implies to say what is and is not good about God. We do not know what is good naturally. So, how can we have judged God? After all tragedy we say why afterwards. So, God created a perfect world to include man and this man has the liberty to choose.

Adam chose to disobey God, sin, death, and suffering became an unavoidable part of life. "When Adam sinned, sin entered the entire human race. Adam's sin brought death, so death spread to everyone, for everyone sinned" (Romans 5:12). The evil in this world is a result of that original sin.

So, I said to myself, "I did not sin, Adam did". But in (Roman 3:23) the bible said we all have sinned. It is natural for us to do wrong. In (James 4:1) it states that evil desires war in us. God gave us principles to live our lives by, morals that are found in the Bible. When we make choices that are different to those absolutes and standards, the result is evil.

Once you surrender your life to Jesus Christ, you enter the major plan, I call it the deluxe plan that God has for you. Rest assure of the promise in his Word, "everything works together for the good of those who love God and are called according to His purpose for them" (Romans 8:28). Sometimes what appears outrageously malicious and tragic can result in something good. My life has not been great throughout the years, Drugs and alcohol played a part of my life that I was not proud of, but I turned out ok now…

When I look back at those years, driving from party to party then pulled up into my driveway and not knowing how I got there the next day. I am surprised that I made it this far. One night, after work I picked up a friend I would occasionally get high with, I had the same suit and tie I worked in, we drove to a drug infested neighborhood, I looked like an undercover detective but did not care, some dealers would not come to the car but there were two guys that signal us. My buddy got out of my car to purchase the drug of choice, I watch him follow a guy to a dark area around a building slightly out of my sight, to purchase the drugs, our defenses were down, before I knew it I saw a flash of light, one of the guys pulled out a gun and shot my friend and took the money. Thank God he shot his leg, it was like a bad dream.

I drove onto the curve he struggled his way into the car and I proceeded to take him to the hospital but he insisted on going to his house, against my better judgement I did as he wanted, praying that he would not die in my car. It seemed like a long 20 minute drive while he was moaning and losing blood, I was unsure of what to do for him, so I tied a piece of cloth I found in the car around his leg to try and stop him from losing so much blood. As I continue to drive fast, whipping around cars trying not to be so suspicious, I looked over and he wasn't moving, he passed out, I hollered "man don't do this"!!!, it was like a movie. Once we got to his house, his family member called an ambulance, everyone was so distracted and out of sort, making disturbing gestures, the police arrived soon after, a police helicopter, and detective cars surrounded his house. The ambulance arrived; the medics were able to help him.

With all this happening and not expecting all the attention, I never seem so disturbed. I made my way over to him on the stretcher and were able to get a story together steering us away from the actual event where it happened and what we were doing.

Looking back, not knowing at that time how good God was then, I was determined then to call it "Good Luck", thinking that this could have been me, it could have been worse, we both could have been killed that night. Today, with the relationship I have with God I know it was God's grace protecting us.

The next morning, I had the task of cleaning up the mess in my car. At the same time keeping this away from my family the guilt was strong, but I knew they suspected something due to my lifestyle.

God allows situations to happen for his glory. He allowed this guy to get shot in front of me. He gave me another reason why I should do the right thing. I had to keep the faith during this storm I had to deal with it because deep down inside God was protecting me repeatedly and I just was not getting it. As I write this passage, tears formed in the wells of my eyes because eventually I did get it. God, I do praise you. Unworthy though I am, Here I am, loved by you.

It took some time; God will take you around the block a couple of times until either you are tired of taking the stroll…or something will break within your soul to do the right thing.

Chapter 13

Fight, Win, Persevere

I have fought the good fight I have finished
The race I have kept the faith
2 Timothy 4:7

Have you ever struggled when your mind tells you to stop, give up, or let go? Have you ever wanted to or attempt to throw in the towel? Life is a struggle when throwing in the towel is not an option what do you do? Fight, Win, and Persevere! Within any battle that we face it is always best to first recognize that we are in a battle. Not knowing that we are in a spiritual battle causing us not to fight and eventually not receive the victory. This fact assists us to face the enemy we do not see or know that it is there.

We must fight back and not give in to temptation and bad habits. We have succumbed to complacency and bad desires, which are our shortcomings. God gives us hope to fight, hope to win and strength to spiritually be committed to victory. We must win the battle against Satan's antics against us. It's important that we put on the coat of armor, the shield of faith, and sword of the Spirit. God resides in the spirit that is in your physical body.

God tells us that we are in a war and that we have spiritual weapons of war at our disposal, they are not physical weapons such as guns and knives, and they will not be affective against the spirit enemy that you cannot see.

Satan has many, many ways to fight you supernaturally therefore the guns will not be effective against the techniques of the Satan.

"(For the weapons of our warfare are not carnal, but mighty through God to the pulling down of strong holds)" 2 Corinthians 10:4

The Scriptures explains that those who "overcome" and persevere in the faith will become heir to eternal life Revelation 2:7 this truth is expressed in Colossians 1:23 where we see that people will be holy, righteous, and above criticism "if they continue in the faith, grounded and unwavering, and are not moved away from the hope of the gospel." All Christians should agree that those who are at last saved are those who do persevere and continue to believe in God's word.

Faith in God's promises is the way we fight the mayhem of the world, the flesh and devil. His Word is filled with his character and all that He is for us. We need to think of the Bible as God's self-revelation. The more we know Him, who He is, what He is like, and what he can do, the stronger our faith grows. Fight the good fight of faith. (1 Timothy 6:12)

As we continue to fight the good fight of faith which means we stand firmly anchored in the word, in the power of the Spirit, imagining ourselves dead to our feelings and, not letting sin run our lives. In the Bible, Peter says: "Therefore, since Christ has suffered in the flesh, arm yourselves also with the same mind, for he who has suffered in the flesh has ceased from sin. (1 Peter 4:1)"

Consequently, we must suffer in the flesh if we are to cease from sin. There will be sufferings in the flesh if we, by the Spirit are to put to death what rises from the flesh so that the lusts are not authorized to rule. Sin rules, and we suffer in our sense of right and wrong if we do not suffer in the flesh. We must fight a good fight not only do we have an enemy to fight, but we must fight a good fight of faith so how do we fight the good fight of faith?

Paul explains to us in Ephesians 6:10-20

> Finally, be strong in the Lord and in the strength of his might. Put on the whole armor of God that you may be able to stand against the schemes of the devil.

For we do not wrestle against flesh and blood, but against the rulers, against the authorities, against the cosmic powers over this present darkness, against the spiritual forces of evil in the heavenly places.

Therefore, take up the whole armor of God that you may be able to withstand in the evil day, and having done all, to stand firm. Stand therefore, having fastened on the belt of truth, and having put on the breastplate of righteousness, and, as shoes for your feet, having put on the readiness given by the gospel of peace.

In all circumstances take up the shield of faith, with which you can extinguish all the flaming darts of the evil one; and take the helmet of salvation, and the sword of the Spirit, which is the word of God, praying at all times in the Spirit, with all prayer and supplication.

To that end, keep alert with all perseverance, making supplication for all the saints, and also for me, that words may be given to me in opening my mouth boldly to proclaim the mystery of the gospel, for which I am an ambassador in chains, that I may declare it boldly, as I ought to speak.

We must fight to keep peace, joy, happiness and to trust in the Lord.

Chapter 14

Forgiveness and Spiritual Growth

In this chapter, I wanted to express how important forgiveness is and how it helps in your spiritual growth. Someone that has done something unappealingly wrong to you and you don't forgive, you stand the chance of being a prisoner of the hurt. We stand the chance of showing bitterness and negativity toward others. Families, best friends, neighbors etc., all over the world go through this. Whether it is a misunderstanding, or a disagreement we stand to be in the defense to prove who is right or wrong. Is it worth it? What do you stand to lose?

It comes a time in our lives that we cannot or should not take forgiveness to our graves because eventually we must answer to God of these shortcomings. We see bitterness and forgiveness in divorces for the most part, when spouses claim of irreconcilable differences, and the hate remains stronger than ever sometimes the hatred is passed down to the children.

Mothers against daughter and fathers against sons, when there seem to be no chance of reconciling of these differences, months, even years pass and nothing has changed, unfortunately we find ourselves at the grave site asking for expired forgiveness. If God forgives us why can't we forgive ourselves or one another?

A couple of months ago, our church was involved in Detention Ministry, Men and women who were incarcerated for many reasons and were soon to be released. They were about to be released to go back in the world and one of the greatest issues they were having were issues of forgiving themselves and others forgiving them. While we cannot control others to forgive, we can work on ourselves, if we ask God for forgiveness, it is done, but we must continue to pray for salvation, pray for and don't pressure our love ones to forgive, sometimes it takes time for others to forgive depending on the circumstances and sometimes they may never will, and that depends on God. So, I tell them, "You must work on yourselves". The relationship you have with yourself is one of the most important relationships in your life besides God. The way we perceive other people is the way we perceive ourselves. We are in a spiritual war and must be vigilant in peace with ourselves and others.

Working on your relationship with God will change your life. We struggle to achieve this and ultimately sabotage ourselves. Studying the word of God will put us in harmony with the Holy Ghost. He can then inspire ourselves to draw upon what we have studied as we teach and lift others up to know God.

As I remember in my teenage years, my father and I did not have a good relationship, I am partly to blame, but I do know it got worst at the end of my teen years into my early twenties this was due to my substance addiction. I remember trying to get along and so did he, but it became worst. We would argue and I would storm out of the house.

I have done some things that I am not proud of which caused confusion, but the result is that I forgive myself, I know God has forgiven me and so has my father. How do I know my father forgives me? When we call one another, we have something to talk about and I am able to say, "I love you Dad" thank you! When I am able to come home on vacation to visit the family, we embrace and have long talks and even go for a drive.

Forgiveness has changed our lives. My mother and father are in their early 80's and One thing I know, you only get one mother and one father in life, in fact you only live once and when you get the chance to hug and talk to your family it is a blessing. Remember God is responsible for giving you life, you must take what God has given and just say, "Thank you".

Chapter 15

Turning Pain into Praise

In John 16:33 which reads, these things I have spoken to you, that in me you may have peace. In the world you will have tribulation; but be of good cheer, I have overcome the world." The scripture takes profound cause in the minds and hearts of so many countless Christians: "In this world you will have trouble. But take heart! I have overcome the world." We must believe that, if we do not believe it, then we will continue to have Pain in our lives. We must turn our pain into Praise.

We've experience heartache and pain in our lives, I know I have. We've struggle with sin daily, observe natural disasters and shocking loss as well. Injustice, brutality, and dishonesty seem to hold dominance. Conflict and difficulty are a commonplace. None of this was God's initial plan for humanity. We fell from our original position in the Garden of Eden.

Nevertheless, When I feel down, I talk to God, it is simple just start talking. I then start to read one of my favorite scriptures like John 16:33 and a few of my others and then this warm feeling of joy come over me, so much that I start to get heated in my praise.

When I think of the goodness of the Lord and how good he has been to me, how much he has blessed me, where he bought me from, how many times he protected me and how he loved me when I did not love myself, all I can do is sing, shout, and dance giving him all praise, all glory and all honor. Whether in my home, my car or in isle eleven at Walmart, I sing to the glory of God, and praise him with no hesitation, why? Because he is Lord. All of us have been hurt by the words from others or we have hurt others by our own words. When you are in pain from hurt and under an attack, turn to the Lord pour out your heart to God. God never wastes our pain, we do that. God has a plan for great purpose and a beautiful future for all who believe in Him. Not despite our past, but because of it.

All the sufferings of the past have prepared me for what I was called to be according to his purpose: A Man of God. I know without hesitation that the pain you are feeling is a valuable instrument that can help uncover your calling and God's given purpose.

I've learned in life our understanding is greater than our experience. When we make a determined preference to refocus painful experiences, we are empowered to shift our perspective, which brings healing, breakthrough, and understanding. Our regrets can be painful, there are many consequences to the choices that you have made in the past, God is always ready to forgive you for your mistakes and help you learn from them. Just be honest with God about your regrets and ask him to help you push further with the peace that only he can give.

Whether we suffer from, health issues, marital problems, incarceration, or day-to-day struggles, we can turn our pain to praise. We acknowledge God in all circumstances because of what he has done for us. We are forgiven. We will receive his timeless inheritance and live without pain. We will always sing his praise in his courts.

Just know that God has accepted you because of Jesus sacrifice for you on the cross, and nothing that you suffer can ever change that fact. Be excited that not only will your suffering not eliminate you from serving God, but the specific ways in which you've suffered can essentially become the greatest ways in which God can use your life to help restore the world.

In this life we will experience pain. God is greater than our pain, bigger than our circumstances. When we trust him, he will exchange our pain for praise. Hand your pain over to God today.

Someone may hurt you for whatever reason, they may not know the damage it causes, or maybe they do know, but you are bigger and better then that, you must be the teacher regardless of the age difference. If God has done all of this work to place us where we are, while giving us all that we have, wouldn't it be a great tribute to God to show him that we've listened, we've learned and it mattered enough to tell somebody the magnitude of his love. Don't waste all what God has given.

Just remember, "Late in the midnight hour God's going to turn it around, it's going to work in your favor"

A Note to the Readers

As this Book strived to unveil and describe speed bumps and acts of my spiritual journey, it would be negligent and thoughtless to close this work without saying thank you to my family who stood by me through my good and bad. Thank you to everyone for your encouragement in ways you just don't know. Thank you for purchasing this project.

Whatever the past has held for us, today I can rejoice that we are able to followship with one another giving each other love and support while we can. We can and will reclaim lost moments short of my walk with God. Nothing has been as delightful as unconditional love for me in the midst of my shortcomings.

Thank you, God, for allowing my words to express your incredible works.

Rev. Michael Gamble

Printed in the United States
By Bookmasters